Appraisal for Medical Consultants -
a handbook of best practice

by Dr Steven Wilkinson and Dr Kwee Matheson

Earlybrave
PUBLICATIONS LIMITED

£12.99

While the publisher and editors have made every effort to ensure that the contents of this publication are accurate, responsibility can not be accepted for any errors.

First published in June 2001

ISBN 1-900-432-29-3

Published by

Earlybrave
PUBLICATIONS LIMITED

Printed in the United Kingdom by
Clifford Thames Printing Limited

Authors:
Dr Steven Wilkinson
Dr Kwee Matheson

Steven Wilkinson is a Senior Research Fellow for the Centre for Organisational Research at Anglia Polytechnic University. His research interests include the use of 'action science' methods in bringing about 'cultural change'. His health service related work includes research into developing Consultant Appraisal models, and delivering training in Appraisal techniques. Steven holds a Doctorate in Education.

Kwee Matheson is Medical Director and Director of Education, and Consultant Anaesthetist at the West Suffolk Hospitals NHS Trust. She has been closely involved with postgraduate medical education in the Trust and in the Anglian Deanery. She is the immediate past Chairman of the National Association of Clinical Tutors, and assisted in the professional development of Postgraduate Clinical Tutors/Directors of Postgraduate Medical Education.

Acknowledgements

Grateful thanks are due to the Consultants from over 15 trusts who have participated in research projects and workshops and attended meetings and whose thoughtful criticism and healthy cynicism is reflected in this book.

Thanks are also due to the Associates and staff of the Centre for Organisational Research without whom much of this work would not have been possible.

The authors acknowledge the work of Dr Paul Ramsey and his team from the University of Washington School of Medicine, Seattle, USA. Dr Ramsey has kindly consented for an adaptation of his 'scale' to be included in this book.

Contents

Chapters

Appendices

The forms presented in the above appendices will be periodically updated and can be downloaded from: www.earlybrave.com

Glossary of Terms

Appraisee

The Consultant being appraised by the agreed process of the appraisal system.

Appraiser

The individual who is chosen by whatever means to conduct the annual appraisal session.

Folder/Portfolio

A file which contains necessary supporting materials for the appraisal and for Revalidation.

Revalidation

The process of renewing a doctors registration on the medical register.

Chapter 1
Background and Introduction

This handbook is aimed predominantly at medical consultants (especially the sceptical) and also at trust management.

There are, so the wisdom goes, two ways in which appraisal should never be introduced:
1. 'Carrots and sticks'; and
2. Via a management down directive.

Welcome to the interesting challenge of consultant appraisal.

The wheel of evolution has brought upon the health industry new demands for accountability and transparency. Many health professionals are already engaging in appraisal as a means of developing practice and managing careers. In such cases, appraisal is not so much a response to a demand as a proactive process.

1

Consultant appraisal works best where it is developed and managed by consultants for consultants as a means of developing professionalism and managing careers. It will not achieve its purpose or work effectively where there is a management imperative or in response to rewards or penalties.

This handbook is written on the premise that anyone reading it is genuinely interested in continuing to develop throughout their professional lifetime.

Why should Consultants be appraised?

Today's patient is better informed, sophisticated and is demanding that doctors be accountable for their practice.

In a perfect world the medical profession would have embarked on appraisal voluntarily and positively before now, to enhance professional development and advancement, and to reassure the public that it is open to peer review. Doctors should not be afraid of using comparisons as opportunities for life-long learning. Ours is not a perfect world and therefore we have appraisal imposed on consultants as part of their contractual obligations (as was the case in England in April 2001) as part of the General Medical Council's (GMC) proposed revalidation process.

It may not seem an auspicious start but if we now manage the appraisal process sensitively and appropriately, it will be of benefit to the profession, National Health Service (NHS) and the public. We hope that this handbook will help you in this challenging task.

What kind of appraisal model would suit consultants?

A model that
● supports the consultant and
● reflects the culture and objectives of the health trust.

There is however no 'off the peg' model. Consultant appraisal will have to be an evolutionary process.

What are the benefits?

Appraisal benefits consultants through:
- Providing an opportunity for career and professional development;
- Reflection and focus;
- Clarifying what is expected of the role of a consultant;
- Recognising service;
- Providing an opportunity to feed back thoughts, views and concerns to management without fear of repression;
- Providing early warning concerning professional issues which may become serious later;
- Support from managers and supervisors;
- The opportunity to make a meaningful contribution by identifying barriers to good clinical practice;
- Contributing to the process of Revalidation.

Appraisal benefits the Trust by:
- Participating in a process that recognises and promotes good Human Resources practice; and
- Introducing quality assurance in line with overall clinical governance.

Chapter 2
Definitions and Perspectives

Instead of stating what appraisal is, perhaps it would be better to start with what appraisal is not!

Appraisal is not assessment or evaluation

Why not?

Assessment involves a review of clinical competencies judged against explicit standards and criteria which would require sophisticated methods of measurement. Evaluation involves making a decision based on the results of the assessment, such as pass or fail. Appraisal can neither be passed nor failed. It is a formative and not a summative process.

Appraisal for consultants should not be hierarchical.

Why not?

Consultants work in a 'flat' structure. Line management is not at the centre of clinical practice.

Appraisal is not a disciplinary or health monitoring process.

Why not?

Appraisal should not overlap or replace existing Trust protocols or management systems. Appraisal does not deal with poorly functioning or under-performing doctors who are correctly dealt through the Trust's disciplinary procedures.

So, what is Appraisal?

Appraisal provides a consultant with the opportunity to meet with a peer to reflect on, and set goals for, professional practice and professional development. It could be viewed as a process of self-assessment and self-awareness underpinned by evidence collected by the individual and drawn from clinical governance.

Although not synonymous, appraisal will contribute to Revalidation. Annual appraisal is not a "mini-revalidation" and needs to be differentiated from revalidation.

The following diagram shows how appraisal, governance and revalidation relate (see figure 1).

Revalidation is an evaluation; a decision is made whether a doctor is revalidated or not. Ultimately, revalidation seeks to establish 'fitness to practice'. The role appraisal will play in this is significant. At appraisal consultants will produce much of the same evidence that will ultimately be used in revalidation. In this way, the same information is being used twice. For appraisal the evidence is being used formatively to develop professional practice and set personal objectives. At revalidation the same information is being used more critically and evaluatively, as in summative assessment.

Figure 1

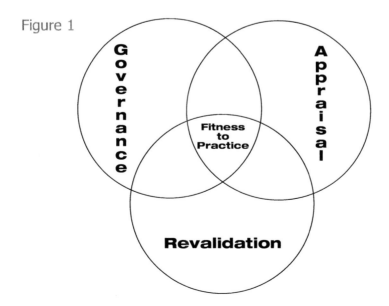

Chapter 3
Establishing a Framework

Let us consider how to introduce the appraisal process. To start with, appraisal needs a framework. A framework for consultant appraisal is the mechanism by which appraisal will be conducted.

Establishing a framework starts with the appointment of a steering group of some kind. Chief Executive Officers are ultimately responsible to ensure that consultants are appraised. They will rarely get involved in the detail of how this is to be done (although in the cases where they do get directly involved, the outcome is most often positive).

A steering group is formed which may involve any combination of the following:

- Medical Director;
- Clinical Directors;
- Human Resource Directors;
- Consultants.

Without question, the most successful trusts have been those that have directly involved the Medical Directors in the steering group.

The next stage in developing a framework is to select a model. There are essentially two models.

1. Ballot and Bank. This model involves forming a bank of appraisers built upon a ratio of one appraiser for every six consultants. The bank is established through a ballot. All consultants are asked to nominate for the bank. An internal election is then conducted. The successful consultants become the first to be included in the bank and should expect to remain in the bank for between three to five years.

2. Line Managers. This model follows the simple formula - Medical Directors appraise Clinical Directors, and Clinical Directors appraise consultants within their departments.

There are arguments for and against either model.

The line management system assumes a hierarchy that does not exist among consultants. In this system Appraisal is linked to job planning and business planning, and risks being seen as a management tool, as performance review (e.g. meeting waiting lists targets), and as a threat to professional development and good clinical practice.

Our experience of 'best practice' favours the Ballot and Bank model. This model is perceived as being more democratic, more about professional and career development and about supporting doctors. Building confidence in the process is a significant success factor to the implementation of appraisal. However, the Ballot and Bank model has been criticised for being separate from job plan reviews and the business planning process, and offers "carrots" but has no "sticks".

Trusts differ in their internal beliefs and values, that is, their "culture" and their structure. Whichever model is developed, it is always best to take this model to the consultant body for general agreement, bearing in mind that not everyone is going to be satisfied with any particular model.

3 items are common to either model.

Portfolio/Folder

Each consultant should have a portfolio/folder for the collection of evidence for appraisal and revalidation. This is discussed in detail in chapter 6.

Appraisal Preparation Form (Appendix 1)

We recommend that the appraisee fills in an Appraisal Preparation Form before the appraisal as an aide memoir so that the appraisal meeting is structured and more focussed, and less valuable time is lost. It must be stressed that this form belongs to the appraisee and is confidential. He/she can choose whether to show it to the appraiser or not before the meeting, and whether it is included in the portfolio/folder.

Appraisal Summary Form (Appendix 2)

At the end of the appraisal, both appraisee and appraiser will agree on the contents of the Summary Form and sign it to signify agreement and the end of that appraisal cycle. This form will contain the appraisee's objectives for the next 12 months. Chapter 8 deals with how to write objectives. One copy will be sent to the Medical Director for filing and one copy will be retained by the appraisee for the next appraisal and as evidence towards revalidation.

The Department of Health (DoH) forms can be found on the DoH web site at:
www.doh.gov.uk/nhsexec/consultantappraisal/consultants.doc

The other aspects of the Framework are administrative and can be easily managed by identifying a responsible administrator, such as the Medical Director's Personal Assistant, and involving him/her in the basics of building, managing and updating an appraisal database. It is up to the Medical Director to link this database to other databases, such as CME/CPD, job plans.

Ultimately, links between appraisal systems become vital when health care trusts introduce team appraisal systems. This will be the next great challenge in cultural change!

Chapter 4
Key Protocols

The protocols are the agreed 'rules' under which the framework will be applied. Like frameworks, these are best developed by a steering group and then worked through with the general consultant body.

There are no rules as to how many protocols must be considered or the scope of what becomes a protocol. The following are examples of protocols developed by consultants for appraisal systems.

Confidentiality

The conversations and documents, which form part of the appraisal process should remain confidential between appraiser and appraisee. The level of confidentiality may need to be defined. Although the interview is confidential, this does not provide protection or sanctuary from law, standing regulations, protocols of clinical governance or principles of Good Medical Practice and the Duties of a Doctor, as decreed by the General Medical Council.

Frequency

Appraisal will be an annual process, although not all issues need be covered in depth every year. For instance, a detailed review of Continuing Professional Development could take place every three years, in line with study and professional leave entitlement – where this entitlement exists. It should be understood how appraisal will contribute to revalidation in determining the content of appraisal from one year to the next. revalidation will occur every five years.

Non Active Consultants

Appraisal is for active practitioners only. Consultants on extended leave or who for whatever reason are not active, should not be required to participate in appraisal until they have been active for an appropriate interval.

Who Conducts the Appraisal?

All those who are to act as appraisers must receive appropriate training, and must be on the medical register. The agreed framework determines exactly who is to conduct appraisals.

Appraisee Choice

In the Ballot and Bank model, an appraisee has the choice of three appraisers. The appraisee makes an appointment with the appraiser. The same appraiser may be used from one year to the next at the discretion of both the appraiser and appraisee. In the line management model, the appraisee has little choice.

Responsibility for Appraisal Outcomes

At the end of the appraisal session, the appraiser and appraisee will complete a Summary Form which should record the appraisee's service and educational objectives for the next 12 months, and concerns (such as Trust resources) affecting his/her ability to deliver the service. One copy of the Summary Form will be filed by the Medical Director, and the other copy to be filed in the appraisee's folder (see page 12).

It is the responsibility of the appraisee to implement the personal outcomes of the appraisal, and the Trust to address the issues raised, as appropriate.

Further Action

If, on conducting the appraisal, it becomes apparent that more detailed discussion and examination of any particular aspect is required, then a follow up plan should be agreed. Either appraiser or appraisee could request further parties brought in to provide expert opinion.

Relationship to Disciplinary Procedures

Matters may from time to time come to light during the appraisal process, which might trigger other procedures. Such matters need to be relayed to the Medical Director, who will act according to extant procedures. Great care must be taken to separate appraisal from any other procedure.

Actions Consequent Upon Appraisal Uncovering Negligence

It may, on rare occasions be necessary to refer the appraisee for further action. This would be necessary where appraisal identifies cases of possible negligence or incompetence. At this point, the issue should be referred to the Medical Director for further action. Careful judgement must determine this kind of action.

Relationship of Appraisal to Ongoing Investigation or Complaints

It is advisable to delay the appraisal if there are serious unresolved complaints or investigations. A consultant whose appraisal needs to be deferred for this reason will, however, in the interim need to continue to have job plan reviews.

Outcomes of investigated complaints may provide evidence useful to appraisal. Discretion regarding the inclusion of complaints into a folder /portfolio remains with the appraisee.

Referral

Any issue that arises within appraisal that is beyond the scope of appraisal or that places the appraiser in a position for which they are not prepared, should be referred to the Medical Director.

Chapter 5
The Appraiser

The appraiser has a unique role to play; for medical consultants the appraiser is a peer and a critical friend. This is in contrast to the appraisal systems within the business sector where the appraiser has a more defined role because Appraisal is linked to pay and promotion and is very much a line management responsibility.

There are some common requirements of appraisers no matter which appraisal model is chosen.

The Prerequisites of an Appraiser

Appraisers must:

- Be on the medical register; and
- Be accountable to the Chief Executive.

Appraisers should:

- Have completed training in conducting appraisal interviews, interpreting evidence and drafting objectives;

21

- Have several years experience at the consultant grade level;
- Be cognizant of current developments about revalidation and CME/CPD;
- Be aware of the appraisal boundaries including confidentiality and the extent of their own roles;
- Be able to differentiate between appraisal and assessment; and
- Understand their responsibilities to patients and to the trust.

Ideally the appraiser should;
- Have an adequate grasp of the appraisee's speciality;
- Themselves have been appraised, but 'buddying' i.e. appraising each other, is not an acceptable arrangement;
- Collect feedback on their appraisal skills in order to learn and improve; and
- Rotate through the bank where this framework has been established.

An Appraiser may decline to conduct an appraisal if:
- They have already done a substantial number (ideal range 6-10 within a 12 month period);
- They believe they are an inappropriate choice;
- They consider they have a lack of rapport with the appraisee; or
- There is an investigation in process.

If the appraiser does not consider that he/she is suitable to appraise a particular consultant, the Medical Director will negotiate a suitable appraiser. Ideally, both parties should be in agreement.

Appraisers and appraisees are colleagues with similar responsibilities and accountability. Where appraisers differ from appraisees is in their specific appraiser training and in their accumulated experience and knowledge. In time, the roles of appraiser and appraisee could be reversed as more consultants are recruited into the rotating bank of appraisers. The appraiser gains invaluable experience over time in how to skillfully conduct a "good" appraisal and in knowing what evidence should be collected for the portfolio/folder. In this way he/she will become a valuable resource within the professional community. Furthermore, appraisers themselves will also develop professionally through this experience; they will learn more about the activities of the Trust and other specialties, and through this shared learning should enhance their own practice.

This will be advantageous to the doctors and to the Trust as the accumulated understanding and knowledge about appraisal grows in step with revalidation which will inevitably become more clearly defined and stringent.

Chapter 6
Evidence

The General Medical Council have established the criteria for revalidation to reflect the seven elements of Good Medical Practice. (Protecting Patients, Guiding Doctors, GMC, London, 1998) Ultimately, appraisal seeks to contribute to revalidation by providing evidence of:

Good Clinical Care

Maintaining Good Medical Practice

Teaching and Training

Relationships with Patients

Working with Colleagues

Probity and Health

Therefore, an appraisal interview will consist of three components:

- A discussion based upon the agreed 'Job Plan';
- A reflective discussion about 'Practice' based on the GMC's Good Medical Practice; and

- A professional discussion which includes Professional Development, Issues or Concerns, and Setting Objectives for the next 12 months.

So, what evidence is required for appraisal?

Appraisal discussions are based upon evidence. The appraisee will collect that evidence relevant to his/her specialty, practice and CPD. Each consultant will have a personalised portfolio/folder within which he/she will collect a range of evidence particular to that consultant. This may include evidence not identified below. It should be acknowledged that it may initially take 2 to 3 years to collect all the evidence, and it will also depend on how comprehensive and accurate Trusts' hospital information systems are.

It remains the responsibility of the appraisee to provide sufficient evidence for appraisal. By the time revalidation is due, most doctors should have sufficient evidence if they start collecting it from their first appraisal.

Job Plan

A current job plan describes what a consultant does and puts the appraisal in context. The job plan should include:

(a) Obligatory professional requirements;

(b) Teaching, mentoring and other commitments;

(c) Non Fixed Session commitments; and

(d) Management Roles and Functions.

The discussion at appraisal is a confirming and interpreting exercise. The appraiser cannot change the appraisee's job plan.

Clinical Practice

This discussion seeks to establish what has gone well and what difficulties were encountered over the preceding 12 months, and to identify issues that may require action to be taken. This discussion should also cover the appraisee's involvement in clinical standards development, education or training, clinical governance and/or research, and the evidence should be discussed in such a way as to encourage self assessment. The Appraisal Preparation Form (Appendix 1) helps structure the discussion.

Many hospital information systems are not yet able to provide accurate information, such as case mix, complications or outcomes. It is essential that any data collected should be from proven robust and valid sources of information. However, any piece of evidence would not be credible on its own; the evidence should be considered as a whole. Evidence may include;

- A personal CV (evidence of qualifications and experience including a record of publications).
- Peer Review, as recorded by meeting agenda, discussion notes, diaries, job plan entries, action plans;
- Data from hospital information systems, such as risk management, work load, complications, outcome, clinical audit and for results from internal auditors;
- Feedback from external audit by Colleges, Deanery and the Commission for Health Improvement (CHI)
- Outcome of investigated complaints; (Note - complaints under investigation should not be discussed at this meeting.)

- Review of outcome of any available patient survey information; (Note - where patient feedback data does not exist a system for collection, collation, analysis and feedback may be discussed along with the resource implications of this process.)
- Letters (compliments and complaints) from the public; and/or
- Feedback from 360 degree surveys.

360 Degree Surveys (Appendix 3 & 4)

Discussion about clinical practice may be supported by feedback from a 360 degree survey.

A 360 degree survey is a device used to collect evidence from those who work with the consultant, such as other medical colleagues, nurses, secretaries and/or theatre staff. Examples of 360 degree surveys can be found at Appendix 3 and 4. A 360 degree survey is a legitimate item of evidence for appraisal as it will yield much of the information required by the GMC under "Good Medical Practice". (See Appendix 3)

The appraisee sends the survey forms to his/her work colleagues. These forms are returned to the appraiser to protect the anonymity and confidentiality of the persons who have filled in the forms. The appraiser will have the results compilated for the appraisee. The appraisee should not see the raw data. It is likely that a protocol for using the 360 degree survey will be needed.

Professional Discussion

To reflect the two-way nature of appraisal, a discussion should take place whereby the consultant has the opportunity to discuss constructively any issue relating to his/her employment including personal goal setting. Evidence may include:

- Personal Development Plan (including resources to support this);
- Continuing Medical Education/Continuing Professional Development diary and certificates (including courses attended, new qualifications and credentials);
- Publication and Research activities including ethics clearance;
- Lectures, presentations; and/or
- Documentation which supports discussion regarding resources or facilities, work practices, personal or patient safety, and grievances or suggestions.

The appraisal preparation form should provide the opportunity for the appraisee to raise the above issues. A summary form should be produced at the end of the appraisal meeting. (See Appendix 2).

Approach to Interpreting Evidence

Since appraisal is about self-assessment, the evidence in the folder is intended to help the appraiser to understand the work of the appraisee. No further interpretation is necessary. However, because the portfolio/folder will also be used in the revalidation process, it is good practice to maintain its content in terms of currency, validity and reliability. Royal Colleges may provide guidance in developing a portfolio.

Chapter 7
Getting the best out of your Interview

So, you have a portfolio, you have an appraisal preparation form, and now you are ready for the interview. Getting the best out of an appraisal interview is a matter of taking a series of initiatives.

Prior to the appraisal meeting contact the appraiser and establish what may be required prior to the meeting. You may want to use this conversation to reassure yourself you have the evidence required in your portfolio.

Decide in advance what it is you want to talk about. You can do this by 'flagging' key issues on the appraisal forms or by sticking notelets into your portfolio. It is not advised to prepare a transcript or narrative. If you have to write something down then 'dot points' are the best way to structure what you want to say.

Make sure you know what it is you would like out of the meeting; you should have already thought about some of your objectives.

These can be talked through and refined if necessary but at least you will have made a start. Word your objectives in such a way as to reflect the service objectives of your team, speciality and the Trust.

Provide realistic solutions to any problems you want to raise at appraisal. A range of solutions is by far more productive than a fist full of problems.

End the appraisal with an agreed summary that reflects your objectives for the coming year and raises any issues that you want the Medical Director to be aware of.

Ensure that the communication loop is complete by following up issues raised at appraisal.

Chapter 8
Objectives and Goal Setting

The appraisee's service and educational objectives are recorded in the Appraisal Summary Form (Appendix 2). Writing objectives requires thought and follows certain rules. Statements that describe aims or goals set by an individual at appraisal are known as Performance Objectives. They can be either:

Outcome oriented – i.e. to be achieved within a time frame e.g. – Complete by...

or

Process oriented – i.e. provides a direction, focus or orientation e.g. – Participate in...

In writing objectives, the fundamental question that must be asked is, 'What do you as the appraisee want to know, do or think during the appraisal cycle'. To this end it may be easier to think of an objective as starting with the unwritten stem,

'During or by the end of this appraisal cycle, I want to be able to...

The words that follow are the Objective.

Five characteristics make an objective meaningful. You can use these to test you objective by asking *'Is it...*:

Measurable?' – can you measure the outcome or participation in the process?

Precise?' – can you be specific? Where are the boundaries?

Observable?' - what is the visual evidence that will indicate you have achieved or are achieving your objective?

Realistic?' – are you aiming too high or too low?

Achievable?' – is there a reasonable likelihood that this can be done?

Objectives say something about consultant *performance*. They don't say anything about what anyone or anything else will do or try to accomplish.

e.g. – *participate in xyz departmental audit.*

In some cases it may be necessary to combine a performance with the key *conditions* under which the performance should or could occur. You may need to describe the tools, equipment, or circumstances that will be a part of the performance.

e.g. – *conduct proposed research into xyz given 'Ethics Committee' approval.*

It may also be necessary to describe the standard of performance. In many cases the standard will be described in terms of a time frame.

e.g. – *complete all registrar appraisals within 7 working days of submission.*

The more complex or ambitious the objective, the more conditions should be included. Compare

work harder – an imprecise, unmeasurable, unobservable, unrealistic and not necessarily achievable statement,
with

reduce surgical waiting list by 50% (performance) given another operating list (condition) within 6 months (standard).

A characteristic of a well written objective is that it begins with a verb. This verb should describe clear and observable behaviours. To 'know' or 'understand' something is neither measurable nor observable. It is necessary to demonstrate knowledge or understanding through quantifiable action. Therefore,

deliver good clinical care

becomes

demonstrate good clinical care (performance) through 360 degree appraisal and governance (standards).

Chapter 9
Barriers and Success Factors

Figure 1 on page 7 shows how appraisal will contribute to revalidation. Appraisal schemes become complicated when they are designed to serve more than one purpose. It seems unlikely that appraisal by itself will be sufficient for consultants to achieve revalidation. The key reasons for this are:

● It has been acknowledged that there is a significant lack of robust and objective data for audit of various sorts
● A reluctance on the part of intended appraisers to be legally responsible for any part in determining a colleague's 'fitness to practice' and;
● A lack of the key resource – time – allocated to conducting annual appraisal.

The disadvantages of a line management framework have been discussed in chapter 3. By employing a speciality specific and Clinical Manager led approach, appraisal risks becoming evaluative.

This would be a mistake. By definition, appraisal is a reflective process aimed at developing individual effectiveness.

Barriers also exist for practical reasons. Lack of staff and inequalities of resource in the National Health Service are significant barriers. Resources needed for appraisal include Consultants' time, space and, in some cases, money. This has not yet been addressed at a national level. Individual trusts have to find the resources for appraisal from within existing allocations. To achieve this in such a way as to not impact on patient care is a challenge.

Other barriers include the perceptions held by consultants that appraisal is being introduced as;

- A 'policing' measure resulting from highly publicised cases of incompetence, misconduct and criminal conduct among doctors;
- A knee jerk reaction by the government anticipating public response to negative media coverage;
- Revalidation - the General Medical Council's response to Government pressure and/or;
- An evaluation of clinical skills.

None of these perceptions are particularly helpful. There is a need for open and honest dialogue between the profession, the DoH, the GMC, and the British Medical Association.

Some trusts experienced success at implementing their own consultant appraisal schemes before a national model was introduced and made compulsory. Providing existing schemes deliver what is required by the DoH and GMC, changes to the system may not be appropriate. Change may have a negative effect by detracting from the consultants enthusiasm with and trust in their own appraisal scheme.

A significant success factor with introducing appraisal schemes is found in the leadership and participation of the Medical Director. By openly participating in appraisal themselves, Medical Directors can break down barriers of resistance.

Some Trusts have engaged in research projects to develop and implement appraisal systems. Other successful appraisal schemes have been introduced by Medical Directors employing a two stage approach. In stage one the aims, objectives, framework and protocols of appraisal are established. This is best done with the involvement of the consultant body, often in a series of interviews and workshops where key issues and concerns can be addressed. It is significant that such workshops identify what is required of an appraiser. In stage two, appraisers are prepared for appraisal. During this stage interview skills are refined, roles and responsibilities are clarified and the mechanism for appraisal is developed.

Success with introducing appraisal systems has been aided by consultants who accept that appraisal provides them with the opportunity for reflection and professional development. Having some involvement in the development of an appraisal system is significant and critical for the process of cultural change. Consultants must be provided with the opportunity to explore the virtues, and to voice their concerns about appraisal. Consultants usually work well together to develop systems and, most importantly, are happier with a scheme they have helped to design and feel ownership of.

Another success factor is appropriate and structured resourcing. It is necessary for trusts to provide resources to lay the groundwork and support the process of appraisal. The key resource is *time.*

Finally, a significant success factor has been the inclusion of 360-degree survey information in appraisal. Such an approach provides specific feedback and promotes valuable discussion at appraisal. It also provides the appraiser with the opportunity to assume more of a 'critical friend' and less of a 'mentor' role.

Trusts that intend to introduce a generic consultant appraisal scheme without seeking consultation with consultants will find resistance. The danger of imposing an external scheme is that consultants will lack ownership of it and it is in danger of becoming yet another meaningless administrative obstacle for consultants to negotiate.

An appraisal scheme should be viewed as the first step in career development that spans the consultant's working life. Consultant appraisal will no doubt evolve in the light of changes in healthcare and politics. The ultimate goal should be to use appraisal to support consultants in professionally developing themselves and their teams so that they can best serve the needs of the public and reduce administrative demands upon their time which prevent them from doing just this!

Appendix 1

NHS Trust

CONSULTANT APPRAISAL PREPARATION FORM

Name	GMC Number
Appraisal Period (year)	Appraisal Date
Speciality/Other Formal Roles	Appraiser

This Appraisal will contribute to Revalidation by providing evidence of MAINTAINING GOOD MEDICAL PRACTICE in the following 7 areas.

1   Good clinical care

2   Maintaining good medical practice

3   Teaching and training

4   Relationships with patients

5   Working with colleagues

6   Probity

7   Health

Receipt of this form is to be regarded as notification that your annual appraisal is now due. Prior to appraisal it will be necessary for both the appraiser and appraisee to prepare. This form is intended to assist in this preparation. This form is confidential and remains the property of the appraisee. However, the decision as to whether your appraiser should have sight of this form prior to the appraisal interview, is to be taken between you and your appraiser. It is suggested that you allow one hour for the appraisal meeting.

Your appraisal will consist of three components
1   *Discussion about your job and Job Plan,* to include service and continuing professional developments.
2   *Clinical Practice.* This will be an evidence based discussion.
3   *Professional Discussion.* This will be a two way dialogue providing you with the opportunity to raise issues, concerns, set goals and generally provide feed back to management.

Below is a checklist to assist you in assembling your Personal Folder or Portfolio. It may not be necessary or appropriate to assemble all the information indicated below as long as your professional and appraisal portfolio is current. (You may wish to refer to the Framework and Protocols for guidance.)

> *Job Plan*
> *Teaching commitments*
> *Obligatory Professional Requirements*
> *Non-fixed sessions*
> *Management Roles and Functions*
> *CV*
> *Career/Professional Development -*
> *Achievements*
> *Audit, Outcome Data and Recorded Complications.*
> *Peer Review*
> *Outcomes of Investigated Complaints*
> *Patient Feedback Survey Information*
> *Royal College guidelines or proformas*
> *Pathways/Protocols Development*
> *360 Degree Feedback*
> *CME/CPD attendance*
> *Research/Publications*
> *Evidence to support discussions around;*
> - *Resources or Facilities,*
> - *Work Practices*
> - *Clinical Standards*
> - *Grievances or Suggestions*
> *Outcome of Previous Appraisal.*

In order to help your appraiser prepare for this appraisal, you may wish to indicate any issue you would like to discuss and provide brief details. Objectives should be realistic and achievable.

Consultants who hold joint appointments with another Trust(s) will have their appraisal at the Trust where their contracts are held, and the Medical Director of the main Trust will send a copy of the Summary Form to the Medical Director of the other Trust(s).

A Summary Form should be completed at the end of the appraisal interview and a copy sent to the Medical Director (and your Clinical Director if he/she is not your appraiser). The original should be filed in your Personal Folder as your collection of evidence required by the GMC for Revalidation.

A Your Job and Role

Is the 'Job Plan' current? **YES/NO**

If **No** - Comment:

Does it accurately describe your duties and responsibilities? **YES/NO**

If **No** – Comment:

B. Last Appraisal

To what extent were your objectives achieved?

Were 'Issues Raised' responded to?

C. Your Practice

1. What has gone well and given you the greatest satisfaction (over the last 12 months)? Professionally, Clinically, Managerially and/or Personally

2. What difficulties have your encountered (over the last 12 months)? Professionally, Clinically, Managerially and/or Personally

3. What issues would you like to address (over the next 12 months)? Professionally, Clinically, Managerially and/or Personally

4. What help do you need to address any of these?

5. What are the clinical standards (e.g. College Good Practice Guides, guidelines, evidence based practice) operating within your clinical area?

6. Tick any of the following areas you have been involved in over the past 12 months
❑ Developing standards of pathways and protocols
❑ Clinical Governance programmes
❑ Education of medical, nursing and other staff
❑ Use of IT in developing service, education teaching
❑ Service Research and development

7. What clinical audit programmes including national programmes have you been involved with over the last 12 months?

D. Professional Discussion

1. What opportunities have there been for you to undertake CPD (including CME)?   (Please list activity during last 12 months)

2. How was this funded?

3. What areas of CPD and service development are of particular importance to you?

4. How do you envisage progressing the above (say over the next 2 years)?

5. What other activities are you involved in as a result of your profession.

E. Summary of Personal Development Plan How do you see your job developing in the next 3 years? What other professional roles, (e.g. education, management, IT, research), do you wish to develop?

F. Additional Comments or Issues you wish to raise at Appraisal

Appendix 2

NHS Trust

| Warning – appraisal does not provide sanctuary from law, standing regulations, protocols of clinical governance or principles of Good Medical Practice. |

CONSULTANT APPRAISAL SUMMARY FORM

This Appraisal Summary Form is completed at the end of the appraisal interview and forwarded to the PA to the Medical Director.

Name	GMC Number
Appraisal Period (year)	Appraisal Date
Speciality/Other Formal Roles	Appraiser

Professional Development objectives for next appraisal cycle (Between 2 and 5 objectives are recommended):

-
-
-
-
-

Issues requiring further action: (This section is not essential)

Appraiser's signature ....Date

Appraisee's signature ....Date

(Note - signatures indicate agreement that these notes are an accurateaccount of this appraisal interview)

Appendix 3
CONSULTANT APPRAISAL 360-DEGREE SURVEY FORM

Introduction

Dr Paul Ramsey and a team from Washington University School of Medicine developed a peer-rating model with the objective of assessing the feasibility of evaluating the performance of practising physicians. The Ramsey model has been referred to by the Revalidation Leads Group of the Academy of the Royal Medical Colleges (01 April 2000) as providing suitable evidence towards the 'fitness to practice' element of revalidation.

The Ramsey model was designed for practising internists in American Hospitals, and therefore, requires some reinterpretation. Notwithstanding this, Ramsey concludes that using this model, it is feasible to obtain peer assessments in areas such as clinical skills, humanistic qualities and communication. It is recommended that 11 responses to this form provides sufficient reliability.

Name ....

Return by Date ....

On the following pages, please rate this consultant in comparison to other consultants with whom you have worked. If you have insufficient contact with the consultant to evaluate him/her on a particular characteristic, circle **U/E (Unable to Evaluate)** beside the item title. Otherwise, Circle one rating response per item. Circle the appropriate number between one and eight where **1** is the lowest rating and **8** is the highest rating.

Responsiveness to Patients				or U/E			
1	**2**	**3**	**4**	**5**	**6**	**7**	**8**
Unresponsive to patients needs and wishes				Very responsive to patients needs and wishes			

Example – U/E indicates that you are unable to evaluate this characteristic. A score of **1** would indicate that this consultant is the worst with whom you have worked in his/her responsiveness to patients needs and wishes. A score of **2** would indicate that he/she is among the bottom few with whom you have worked in this characteristic. Conversely, a score of **7** would indicate that this consultant is among the best with whom you have worked in his/her responsiveness to patients needs and wishes. A score of **8** would indicate that this consultant is the best with whom you have worked in this characteristic.

Respect				or U/E			
1	2	3	4	5	6	7	8
Does not respect the choices and rights of other persons regarding medical care.				Respects the Choices and rights of other persons regarding their medical care			

Medical Knowledge				or U/E			
1	2	3	4	5	6	7	8
Limited, fragmented and not current.				Extensive, well integrated and current.			

Diagnostic Skills				or U/E			
1	2	3	4	5	6	7	8
Very poor ability to diagnose and treat patients				Excellent ability to diagnose and treat patients			

Clinical Care				or U/E			
1	2	3	4	5	6	7	8
Very poor standards of clinical care. Does not recognise the limits of his/her competence. Puts patients at unnecessary risk				Very high standards of clinical care. Practises always within the limits of his/her competence. Ensures that patients are not put at unnecessary risk.			

Integrity				or U/E			
1	**2**	**3**	**4**	**5**	**6**	**7**	**8**
Lack of professional conduct, honesty and trustworthiness.				Always shows professional conduct, honesty and trustworthiness.			

Psychosocial Aspects of Illness			or U/E				
1	**2**	**3**	**4**	**5**	**6**	**7**	**8**
Does not recognise or respond to psychosocial aspects of illness.				Recognises or responds to psychosocial aspects of illness.			

Management of Multiple Complex Problems				or U/E			
1	**2**	**3**	**4**	**5**	**6**	**7**	**8**
Very limited ability to manage patients with multiple complex medical problems.				Excellent ability to manage patients with multiple complex medical problems			

Compassion				or U/E			
1	**2**	**3**	**4**	**5**	**6**	**7**	**8**
Shows inadequate appreciation of Patients' and families' special needs for comfort and help, or develops inappropriate emotional involvement.				Always appreciates Patients' and families' special needs for comfort and help, but avoids inappropriate emotional involvement.			

Responsibility				or U/E			
1	**2**	**3**	**4**	**5**	**6**	**7**	**8**
Does not accept responsibility for own actions and decisions; blames patients or other professionals				Fully accepts responsibility for own actions and decisions.			

Problem-Solving				or U/E			
1	**2**	**3**	**4**	**5**	**6**	**7**	**8**
Fails to critically assess information, risks, and benefits; does not identify major issues or make timely decisions.				Critically assesses information risks and benefits; identifies major issues and makes timely decisions.			

Communication with colleagues				or U/E			
1	**2**	**3**	**4**	**5**	**6**	**7**	**8**
Does not inform colleagues when sharing care of patients Unwillingness to consult colleagues.				Keeps colleagues well informed when sharing of patients Always consults colleagues when necessary .			

Working in teams				or U/E			
1	**2**	**3**	**4**	**5**	**6**	**7**	**8**
Does not take responsibility for ensuring that the team provides care which is safe, effective and efficient				Takes responsibility for ensuring that the team provides care which is safe, effective and efficient.			

References

Ramsey Dr P.G. et al (1993) Use of Peer Ratings to Evaluate Physician Performance, in JAMA, Vol 269 No 13.

Leadership				or U/E			
1	**2**	**3**	**4**	**5**	**6**	**7**	**8**
Poor teamleader: Makes no effort to ensure that the whole team is polite, responsive and accessible and effective service. Does not lead by example				Outstanding team leader: Does his/her best to make sure that the whole team is polite, responsive and accessible and effective service. Leads by example			

Health				or U/E			
1	**2**	**3**	**4**	**5**	**6**	**7**	**8**
Neglects his/her own health to the detriment or endangerment of patients.				Does not neglect his/her own health.			

Teaching				or U/E			
1	**2**	**3**	**4**	**5**	**6**	**7**	**8**
Does not demonstrate the skills, attitudes and practices of a competent teacher. Poor supervision of students and junior colleagues.				Demonstrates outstanding skills, attitudes and practices of a competent teacher and makes sure that students and junior colleagues are properly supervised			

OVERALL Clinical Skills				or U/E			
1	**2**	**3**	**4**	**5**	**6**	**7**	**8**
Very poor overall clinical skills				Outstanding overall clinical skills			

Strunin Professor L (2000) *How the Royal Colleges and Faculties might Contribute to the Process of Revalidation*, Revalidation Leads Group of the Academy of Royal Colleges

Appendix 4

CONSULTANT APPRAISAL 360-DEGREE SURVEY FORM

Consultant being appraised ("appraisee"): ....

All NHS staff are being appraised as part of continuing professional development. Your perspective would be much appreciated as we begin to develop appraisal for consultant staff. The appraisee will send you this form. Your identity will be kept **confidential** as you cannot be identified and only the appraiser will view this form.

Appraiser: ....

Please return the form to the appraiser in the enclosed envelope.

What is your opinion
1. of the doctor as a team player?

2. of his/her communication skills?

3. of his/her attitude towards patients and staff in your area?

4. of his/her punctuality

5. of his/her skills as a teacher and trainer

Does he/she gives you cause for concern?

Additional comments:

Comments about the form and process:

Thank you for your assistance.

The forms presented in the above appendices will be periodically updated and can be downloaded from: www.earlybrave.com